AF411798

MONICA

MONICA

ARNOLD KLEIN

SAN FRANCISCO
BROWNTROUT PUBLISHERS

First published in the United States of America by
BrownTrout Publishers, Inc.
Post Office Box 280070
San Francisco, California 94128

Library of Congress Catalog Card Number 94-078405
Copyright © 1994 Arnold Klein
All Rights Reserved.
Printed in the United States of America

ONE

MONICA

"I only count the happy hours" is the mot
Insculpted on a sundial, and it's apropos,

Since dials only function on those pleasant days
When the sun is shining brightly; and a darker phrase

Was chosen by a learned doctor to adorn
The mechanical contrivance he would wind each morn:

"The night is coming shortly!" — this in self-critique,
To mind him of his indolence, and of his Greek.

Now I waive the question, what a man might stress
Appropriate to other, more precise, or less,

Methods for the measurement of time of day,
Water in a dribble, atoms in decay,

Or the sequent oscillations of a tuning fork,
To ask, What motto best befits besieged New York?

For this island city is a sundial too,
And though it lies perhaps a few degrees from true

And its avenues and cross-streets only match the ruts
Of accidental nature, there is one that cuts

So perfectly its lamps are like a sundial's pins,
And it's with someone leaning there our tale begins.

Now the fellow who was leaning on the lamp that spite
The high mean sun of summer blazed electric light

ARNOLD KLEIN

As if so keen to better its celestial twin,
Was a gentleman of thirty, trig, and spruce, and thin,

Perhaps a little fussy as regarded mode,
With kidskin leather pumps and gauzy socks that showed

A dandy's yellow riblet just below a cuff
Of worsted wool as flaccid as a bloodhound's scruff,

A jacket made to order, and of such a drape
The air itself was emulous to match its shape,

And beneath this dapper vestment there were limbs as neat,
And the tawny of his moustache matched his kid-clad feet.

And yet the man was clinging to the streetlamp's trunk,
A posture sorting less with dandy than with drunk;

A bearing that bespoke an indecisive mind —
Hardly a surprise, for you can often find

That trepidatious contradictions interpose
Between the mind and flesh, no less the mind and clothes.

"Women!" he was thinking (for it falls to me
To overhear his thoughts, as well as oversee),

"If only we could do to them what chemists do,
And make an assay of their parts with gas or goo,

Or better, with electrodes pry apart their souls,
And match the plus and minus to the proper poles!

MONICA

What qualities would crowd to the negating side
But vanity, manipulation, pets, and pride,

Affectation, greed, back-biting, reprimands,
Snares and tests and expectations and demands!

A Faraday in womankind must count in vain
The vices in the vices that their souls contain;

Yet Faraday himself," and now he left the pier,
"Would marvel how such souls, all minuses, cohere!"

Perhaps you think this incoherent and uncouth,
Consorting badly with his clothes, itself, and truth;

I'm not a fop myself, logician even less,
Incapable of judging truth as judging dress,

But I'm a virtuoso and a connoisseur
Of mental states, and this one was, believe me, pure;

Faulty by the scale of taste, perhaps, and sense,
But, in terms of passion, sheerest eloquence.

For Clavering (the fellow's name) had lately done
With a very sour romance, which he had begun

Just the month before, as he began the rest,
With hopes of blessèd love, and marriage, also blest;

Nor was he so unlikely as a friend or mate,
For lofty social status and a manse upstate,

ARNOLD KLEIN

Millions in the bank, and millions more ahead,
Were, in that luxurious day (now, thank God, fled),

Powerful inducements, maximal constraints,
Not only on a woman's heart, but on a saint's.

Still, he never prospered — neither loved nor wed.
There was something wrong. But what? And where? In bed?

Vicious speculation! Not, for that, untrue;
Clavers knew his defects, but he also knew

The universal verdict that the world admits
Is often just a whisper grown concrete by bits,

Until it's hard to tell which is effect and cause.
We heard what Clavers said of women — are those flaws

Mere imagination, or had he, by hap,
Met only such as gave the rumour life, and sap?

At all events it seems now that he's broke the bands
Of old obsession, and, if we had freer hands

(For moral claims encumber us, whom truth entreats),
We'd show him cleaving mist, not traffic, seas, not streets;

For though we live in shrunken times, when our foes
Are only our familiar friends, or selves, their blows

Are real enough, and I protest whoever slays
His lover, or his doubts, deserves heroic lays.

But note the very figure that our hero chose
Remains a little dark — electric current flows

Between a minus and a plus, and Maxwell proves
Attractive fields arise whenever current moves;

And Clavers, having crossed Broadway at speed, now spies
Office workers' knees and lady joggers' thighs.

His pace abates, resolves recede; at last a tree
Offers him a point of view, and *point d'appui.*

"Is there anything more lovely than a woman's legs?"
He asks himself, "and where does it reside," he begs,

"This loveliness, that keeps unchanged, despite its forms,
Its essence, yet admits of neither laws nor norms?

Or is there some ideal, from whose domain derives
A recollection of our ante-natal lives

Present still as redolence or residue,
And prompted by the knee and ankle, thigh and thew?

And we distribute censure, or perfection vault,
By swift, unconscious contrast with this old gestalt,

This abstract ur-expression of consummate form,
Still visibly invariant amid this swarm?"

Two speeches now of Clavering's — perhaps you find
The fellow of pedantic and insipid mind?

And yet each thought is vital, and concludes in deeds.
More: pedantic speculation often leads

To acts of high creation; and the present case,
Despite its carnal tincture, has an abstract base:

For Clavers was a reading man, and he had read
A certain Latin sage who, from a Greekish head,

Argued as a paradox that truest wealth
Cannot be lost or squandered, or removed by stealth;

A noble thought, to which, a pauper, I assent,
But one that clearly turns on what the fellow meant

By wealth, which here, as you have guessed, imports The Good,
And must be something inward. So a lover should,

Thought Clavers, shun the mere physique — indeed dispense
Even with the lover, that caprice of sense!

Hurrah for Clavering! — But how does this agree
With his taste for women's legs, and his misogyny?

And how explain the leaning fear, the loud disgust,
That vitiated doubts till supervening lust

Brought him to a standstill? And what might be the goad
That kept him crossing back and forth, till evening glowed

And made the city not a sundial, but the bars
An astrologue might use to measure sweeps of stars?

At last he moves from avenue to cul-de-sac,
Windowless and grimy, save where one gold plaque

Glimmers in the moonlight, of exquisite work.
Clavers lights a match and reads it: WILLIAM BURKE.

TWO

A*nrennen gegen Sprachgrenze!* — Well, let's grant
We know what language can perform, and what it can't;

We know its pictures of the world are all we've got;
We know it's not a cage, but do we know why not?

Ingenious engineers have so designed our zoos
The animals are fenced, but bars don't block the views;

Instead, concealed to men, deep slanted pitfalls gape.
And that's what language is: no bars, but no escape,

And to run against its limits is like being hurled
Into space, not silence, from its picture-world.

The queasiness attendant on that drop can blanch
Even those who reach the edge and stop. I'm stanch,

But much prefer to lure things up, than look, or leap.
So follow Clavers to a workshop, where a heap

Of test tubes, quadrants, canvas, scores and skulls conveys
Vague outlines of the figure of the man I'd raise.

A figure like a mountain, but whose hand was such
As added the musician's to the surgeon's touch;

In beard and breadth a bear, but whose deep-seeing eyes
Suggested mind to match his deftness and his size.

Calderón delBarca baffled, with these clues,
Both pagan sage and demon: what's all grasp, all views?

ARNOLD KLEIN

His Age of Gold said God, but in this age of dark
Is pluripuissant Burke enough? Or Polyarch?

The word that might have answered — artist — has a buzz
Disgusts me more than looking down that pitfall does;

And only names new-coined can capture one at ease
With math, genetics, economics, plants, disease,

Syriac, computers, physics, fugues and suites,
Who drew like Leonardo and could dream with Keats.

You think I overstate his skills. Reserve your doubt;
Recall that it was Clavering who sought Burke out,

And Clavers must be granted, I don't say restraint,
At least a perfect judgement of his own complaint,

And something so diversivolent's past the ken
Of unitechs, and solomaths, and monomen.

Still, the contrast of the two was such as might provoke
Mere disbelief in cynical or shallow folk.

What mortar of a complot could compound and fuse
A man of lust and gold to one all grasp, all views?

Nothing so bizarre, believe me; one way, bland;
For Clavers had the pockets, Burke the mind and hand,

And no one needs instruction how those three accord.
But on another level — I'm amazed, I'm awed

At their joint audacity, and I confess
I'd have quailed when Burke asked "No?" But Claves said "Yes!"

And with that word an undertaking was begun
That showed how these two men were, more abstractly, one:

For what it was that Clavering had asked of Burke
Was *to fashion him a woman and to make her work.*

An artificial woman! Do you applaud or hiss?
I think a moral poll would find two sides, on this.

Aesthetically, however, savor how it bends
All of Burke's abilities to Clavers' ends.

Notice: artificial; that is, Burke's own sphere.
Notice: work, not live; for it was Clavers' fear

(And not so wholly baseless as you might believe)
That something that could move and act might up and leave.

But baiting that, the boldness of the scheme astounds,
Though some sophisticates demur on worldly grounds.

Desire's quickly blunted when the girl is real;
How can a doll restore, no less maintain, its zeal?

Sophisticates beware! For you at once asperse
Burke's talents in this area, and, what is worse,

Desire's own desires miss, who fail to know
Reality's its deepest, nay, its only foe,

And comprehends the others — other, self, and time.
But fantasy alone is something less than mime,

So Clavers planned his doll to be a dream-in-sense,
And left it up to Burke to give it permanence.

My personal objection to their common cause
Has less to do with blunted zeal than Newton's laws.

That action and reaction are the same, reversed;
That, for things to move, a force must function first;

That bodies, whether moving or at rest, resist,
Are lectures that the lover reads the physicist,

And blast me if I see how plastic, paint and mesh
Are freer from the laws that govern force, than flesh.

But Clavers would declare this remonstration vain:
The stubbornness of bodies lies within the brain,

And brain was what the doll would lack — a neural waste;
Another thing, perhaps, to pique a worldly taste.

The two rehearsed the details of the doll once more,
And something queer occurred, and had occurred before:

Clavers felt obliged to take the Master's line
On an undecided detail of the doll's design.

Now Clavers has a kind of dim Platonic streak
Which Burke, by dialectic art, could tap, or tweak,

MONICA

And gradually, from having ruled the works within,
The Polyarch annexed the puppet's shape and skin,

Till finally in everything he took the lead
And carried all the points on which they disagreed.

This last debate is typical of Clavers' case.
Concerning the masseter of the motion's face

(For though in some respects the doll departed from
Actual anatomy inside, in some

Aspects, as the muscles that affect physique,
Burke would stoop to plunder nature's own technique),

Clavers argued that, although the law held good
That form should follow function, facial muscles should

Their saliency abandon, lest their partial line
Contravene, or supersede, the hyperfine

Expression of emotions, which must be their head.
But William Burke replied: "That law of form is dead.

Its paradigm of function was the old machine.
A house is meant for living. But what does living mean?

The Devil take all simplifiers! — That's for art.
In organisms, nature, giving every part

A manifold of functions, pretty much declines
To use your teleologies in its designs.

ARNOLD KLEIN

The muscle you would sink is one of three that raise
The lower jaw in grinding. Surely grinding weighs

For something? Or is grinning more esteemed than food?
The temporal and pterygoid alike elude

Notice, though a practiced eye remarks the first.
Beauty is a manifold revealed; reversed,

This truth yields simplify and hide. I augment;
Will show the three in one — that is, with your consent."

One hardly knows oneself how to resist this bid,
Although one has, one hopes, more sand than Clavers did.

It's cogent, it's perspicuous, it's — or is it true?
Is comeliness a concentrate or residue?

I think Burke skimps the adventitious-undesigned,
The beauty from above, the beauty from behind,

The beauty of bare knees below the table top,
The beauty of crossed thighs that dovetail as they drop,

The beauty self-forgot of hinder hems of shorts,
Unconscious comeliness... But acid Burke retorts

Such revelations multiply as thoughts abate,
Until at last the graceful and the mindless mate. —

Kleist's argument, of course, of puppets and of gods.
But Clavers "quite agrees," and with like civil nods

Had yielded to the Master on the hair and hips,
Breast and buttock, weight and waist, knees, eyes and lips,

As well as quasi-mythic things, and things abstruse,
The Bone That Has No Name, the bone the Jews call *Luz,*

And some declare the seedcase of a ghost; in short,
A million strands that only Burke could see or sort,

And if the doll diverged a little or a lot
From Clavers' first imagined image, well, so what?

The thing was meant to fill a void in Clavers' heart,
And Burke was no mere tradesman, hired for the part;

The Polyarch was solitary, rich, and proud,
And would have called it quits at once if crossed, or cowed.

Discussions ended, Clavers leaves. His fancy, numb,
Labors for an image of the doll-in-sum;

But had his senses been a little less extinct,
He might have seen a picture, taken, made, or inked,

Half-hidden on the desk top, that had done the work,
And showed him what was really in the mind of Burke.

THREE

MONICA

Psychologists agree that infant minds engage
This outer world of limitation stage by stage,

That wish fulfillment in the womb is balked at birth,
Then checked by space and time, and wrecked by dark and dearth,

Until we call that babe a babe no more, who learns
Reality and pleasure are opposed concerns.

Psychology's a modern field, with many sects.
But older philosophic thinking still directs

Its squabbles as to starts and stops, and swerves and norms.
One moves from schemes of action into abstract forms,

And having split the mind and body from the start
Thinks himself arrived at truth, and not Descartes.

Piaget, avaunt! And Freud and Adler, who
Disagree wherever Hegel and Nietzsche do,

Like them hate arrested motion, which they stress
By saying those who move this process back "regress."

I never use that word myself. It's really bad
To stigmatize returning to the world we had!

If only each became a child in his/her soul,
If only he/she were free from shame, if only whole,

If only we could live in peace... Don't you agree?
Or do you find too much *if-only* here, like me?

ARNOLD KLEIN

But Margie Leighton, from whose mind this mead we sip,
While she puffs and struggles with her art school scrip,

Her plastic casket filled with hammers, paint and pen,
Her massive folio that daunts the strength of ten,

But which she subways every day from Brooklyn in,
Though it made, if anything, a creed too thin,

And would add if-only's with each coil and wrench
She musters for her labors at her lonely bench.

For whether Marge called children true, or just unbent,
Was largely ruled by how her morning classes went;

And mostly, and with cause akin, they ended ill,
For Margie's teachers valued only market skill,

And of that market targeted the largest part,
While Margie, with her child's eyes, distrusted art,

Hated economics, considered school malign,
And aimed between the primitive and infantine.

Hard training for a jeweller! — Not the worst, perhaps;
For, as Margie takes her hammer, tears, and taps,

We see her faith expand with every stud she blunts,
As if the mirrored wall before her served at once

To multiply her mettle and her person, too:
If only people wouldn't mock whatever's new,

MONICA

If only teachers listened to the things you said,
If only students didn't try to get ahead,

If only myth instead of math were taught in schools,
If only women ruled the world, if only tools

Weren't so expensive — are these so unsound?
Disparate maybe, but they unite around

One doctrinal polarity, for all suppose
A uniform if multi-sided set of foes,

A principle that's clear enough, if you bestride
The working-white-male-woman-hating-Western side;

And though I see a different union manifest,
For Margie's thoughts all fail my own if-only test,

If only students came to learn and not to judge,
If only hearts could pump their way through social sludge,

If only myths had other roots than human minds,
If only gender roles conformed to moral kinds,

If only children weren't, as Augustine claims,
Horrible epitomes of crimes and shames,

If only — well, there's one I can't refine away:
If only Marge were not as lovely as the day!

Now judged against a norm, or taken limb by limb,
Margie, who was clumsy, short, and hardly slim,

ARNOLD KLEIN

With little knees a-peep from cut-off coveralls,
And wild archaic hair that fountains as it falls,

In hue and hand like husk, and eyes of blue-green grain,
Like sleeping granite dreaming of the glacier's reign,

Or, in dawn, distress, or wonder, or in love,
Like the stone awaking with the ice above,

May not have been considered pretty or well-knit,
But not because she didn't form or failed to fit;

Rather it's the failure of what Kohler rates
The Error of Experience, whereby the traits

That appertain translocally to total fields
Are sought in and-sum aggregates, neuronal yields;

A notion we can put in stage and process terms,
Since what we grasp as wholes we also grasp as germs

(Which shows that Kohler's party, turning back the clock,
Rests as much on Goethe as it does on Mach),

And Marjorie's especially a case of that,
Since her hardly slim was really baby fat,

Her post-instruction pouting really baby-pets,
And in her head not only baby thoughts and threats,

But also, by a freak, two vestige baby teeth;
All of which exacerbates the charm beneath

MONICA

Of a beauty not yet finished, yet withal complete,
Till "lovely as the day" is no inane conceit.

Too much triple sec perhaps? It's not her fault;
Life will soon enough provide the lime, and salt.

Perhaps it's even started, for as Margie weeps
Her mind of hydromel reveals both dregs and deeps;

For Marjorie's no dreaming fool, ideals apart;
She's middle-class, and school (and even schools of art)

For her is hardly dorms and dates. It's all expense:
Tuition, loans, equipment, hunger, books and rents.

Now though I know that eighteen and a half to some
Is old enough to sicken in a Brooklyn slum,

Too young to take a taxi, just the age to drudge,
I own I feel for Marge a superstitious nudge

Of casual compassion, which almost blows
My grudging her her youth, and welcoming her woes.

But what it is distresses Marge the most, I think,
And gives her greeny eyes their novel veins of pink,

Is neither class critique nor miserly routine,
But notice simultaneous from Dad and Dean

That a season's leave-of-absence might at once redress
Her economic plight and academic mess.

ARNOLD KLEIN

Reality's "recalcitrant" — it kicks you back!
Those brilliant psychoanalysts who all attack

Regression didn't reckon with the word's root-source.
Get kicked or back away? Why, back away, of course!

The infant, after all, whose pleasure's checked employs
Shifts, as sounds and gestures, to restore its poise;

Weeps, and wiggles, and it works; and this reveals
Why grown-ups still resort — regress — to such appeals.

Now speech is sound, and words employed to please sublime
In poetry, as gestures do in craft, and mime;

For arts are just the latest stage of infant shifts;
And just how much of magic thinking making lifts

From infant squirms behold, for what Ms. Leighton pops
From its little shaping swages, buffs, and strops,

Is not a pendant, but a world, and she its Thor;
Do babies at the breast, or in the womb, have more?

But worlds of one's own making evanesce at last.
Margie takes her finished oval, clips it fast

To a bone and feather earring, wipes her eyes,
Rolls her cut-off denims further up her thighs,

Packs her kit and goes. She can't afford to sob;
She's middle-class, remember, and she needs a job,

MONICA

And within the hour has an interview.
I think she'll make a bold impression there, don't you?

For as her smudgy fingers wiped away her tears
They marked her savage cheekbones with two crimson smears.

Are baby teeth so innocent? Or do we find
That infancy and appetite are oft combined?

FOUR

The sensory, phenomenal and conscious field
Of different sorts of animal remains concealed.

The umwelts (as the experts say) of eyeless worms
Or giant fulmars floating on the southern therms

Or of the star-nose mole who haunts the swaley banks
Or coelacanths who tilt their hoary leg-like flanks

To wring from lightless seas the least electric charge
Or platypi who burrow at the river's marge,

Though clear enough to others of their kind, defy
Our efforts to embrace them. Now I ask you why

People baffle people, if they all possess
Similar sensoriums and consciousness?

The answer tells how poorly our pretensions show.
For people don't have umwelts — they have egos, though,

As those who see the city from the streets confirm,
For there's another city hid behind the berme,

A world within each quiet block, of yards and flats,
Unknown to urban swells, but not to bugs and rats.

You wonder how the rich endure the urban churn?
Borrow of the roach his brinkless world, and learn.

Now whatever is the case among the toffs uptown,
Here below, you sometimes see, between two brown

ARNOLD KLEIN

And weathered walls of brick, a kind of metal grill
Locked and barred, and crowned with such sharp wire fill

As makes you bleed to see it; and that door traversed
A tunnel leads to one less gracious than the first,

But open that and find a manse — a cricket pitch,
A putting-green, perhaps, and fruiting arbors rich!

So what, if all around, as in some Black Hole hell,
The dead slums only stand because they lean so well?

So what, if toddlers, woozily on sills unbarred,
Eat a lead paint lunch and dully eye the yard?

Confess: your conscience quivered with this cheap appeal,
Especially that business with the lead paint meal;

But our tale is other, for instead of slums
Our mansion's ringed by flats at let for lavish sums,

Its open acre offers such a bragging view
The landlord asks, and gets, a price beyond his due.

You've guessed his name, of course. Remove his cashmere stole
He's little changed, although his friends would find that droll:

He hasn't lost his heart in over half a year.
He's thrived, but don't expect his closest friends to cheer;

They'll never pardon him the fun they've lost, and treat
His coolness with as much contempt they did his heat.

But Clavers' nonchalance has corresponding boons.
He's now the target of coquettes, whom he repugns.

It's not that he can boast a heart of proof above
The ways of wedlock and the world. Oh no; it's love,

For what at present's circuits, gears, and plastics soft
Scattered on a workbench in a Bond Street loft.

Here's perversity, you're thinking. While we wait
For Burke to finish up, however, let's dilate

A little on this question of perversity.
Observe that our instance subdivides in three:

It's in pieces; it's a doll; it isn't done.
But where exactly does this jump the normal run?

Can't anticipation overwhelm events?
Ain't imagination sovereign over sense?

Don't body parts stir lust? Perverse? It's almost prim:
He loves what he imagines has been made for him.

Now Burke had kept his client off through sheer disdain,
Partly out of pride, and partly to sustain

A certain private plot, but mostly, I surmise,
From love of ostentation and the cheap surprise:

For Clavers often called or came for Burke's report,
And with a sigh, a sneer, a silence or a snort

ARNOLD KLEIN

Burke could fashion vague frissons of joy or dread
Without referring once to how things really sped.

An afternoon in April closed this masquerade,
When Burke, who had for months let Clavers languish, laid

The doll upon his doorstep, rang, and took his leave.
Now many things miscarry in this world to grieve,

Which was why the Polyarch preferred his own;
For Clavers never heard, and thus all day, alone,

In running shorts disguised, the doll remained in place.
Clavers saw its shadow first, then its face

Through the fish-eye peephole, with its fine effects,
Then above the chain with which the man protects

Access to his home. Who could this stranger be?
A little cross-inquiry proved that *this was she.*

Consternation changes to delighted squirms.
Such loveliness and life! — Such unexpected terms!

Our hero pulls it in and lifts it up the stairs
To a locked-door suite, and from its knapsack tears

The tome that tells him how it works; and while he reads
I must confess the word I've used throughout misleads:

For "doll" implies a blow-up toy in porno pits,
A vile vulgar travesty with painted slits,

A cheap misshapen lump to heat the fools and lost.
But dolls like that don't cost a million two, or cost

A mastermind eleven months of pains to make,
Or seem so real that Clavering believes it fake,

And, to flush the living person miming there,
Resorts to brutal probes no sentient thing could bear.

A queerish first encounter — pinches, pokes and slaps,
But one that rather slows, than hastens, faith, perhaps;

For every local change, however small and sole,
Reacted realistically upon the whole,

Which, in turn, reacted on our hero's zeal,
And answered unequivocally, *the doll was real.*

A finger bent — knees flex, the shoulders sink and rise;
A finger wrenched — imploring looks and wordless sighs;

A finger stroked — limbs slacken, eyelids droop, quick pants;
A finger sucked — lascivious erotic trance;

A finger bit, first joint — an algolagnic hiss;
Second joint, left hand — must I go on with this?

The manual was seven pounds, and quite succinct;
The doll could boast eleven thousand keys, crossed-linked;

Which gave it something like a trillion trillion cues.
Splendid thing for Clavering — disturbing news

ARNOLD KLEIN

To philosophic thinkers, who accept as law
The Maker Knows The Made, and these conclusions draw,

That, as all-creating God, as perfect mind,
Made and knows the universe, so humankind

Makes and knows its products; for a trillion ten
Was where the maker's work crept past the maker's ken,

And maybe made the realms of art and nature mate —
That is, if such lability's a human trait.

Now Clavers, as the doll's infinitudes unfold,
Declares it liker life than anything ensouled.

It's never twice the same, and though it still obeys
He finds it always does so in surprising ways.

He even thinks it lifelike where it outstrips flesh:
Its threaded muscles, lacking nerves and sense, stay fresh

Whatever crabbed position his caprice ordains.
Nay, he even thinks so when he cleans the drains,

Through the central tank in which they end their route,
By opening, like double doors, the buttocks out.

This sentiment of animation only grows
When Clavers tires of it nude, and buys it clothes.

To fill its many closets is a sweet despair.
How flaunt its slender frame, set off its blood red hair?

MONICA

How tight the butt and bodice, low the backless shirt,
High the hem and heel, and bagged the shorts and skirt?

Perhaps this was the keenest pleasure too. Whyfor?
The body underneath would seem to count for more,

And clothes be only relative to what they hide.
And yet we find it's almost always clothes decide,

Some say as needful augments to our sense-confines,
Incapable unaided of perceiving signs

Of sexual intention, some say to offset
Our lack of mating themes, as antlers, plumes or sweat,

Momentous maladaptions that in turn bestowed
Darwinian advantage on the man-of-mode.

Myself, I make banality the human par,
Which ever-changing clothes conceal, but don't debar;

But since the ever-changing doll evades this vice,
I say that Clavers, clothing it, has blundered twice,

First for having made the banal his ideal,
Then for having treated that as merely real;

And add, if something human was the goal he set,
He should have stuck with that unchanging porn pit pet.

To name his perfect lover is the final sport.
Lydia? Linda? Lisa? — Well, to cut it short,

ARNOLD KLEIN

Angela, or Angie, was the name he found
For one we leave apparelled, pampered, named, and — bound.

A curious world a mole must have, who makes for dark!
And stranger still the coelacanth's, who hunts a spark;

The worm that tastes the earth, the bird who never lands,
And platypi with webs and bills and poison glands!

But strangest is the world, I say, of men's conceit;
For other eyes were witness to that doormat meet,

And gloated on that face possessed and figure lean,
So lovely, lively, lifelike — life-unlike, I mean!

FIVE

Of all the pieties perhaps the most enshrined
Is The Influence Of Greeks Upon The Western Mind.

Shelley said they rule our present from their pasts;
To Whitehead our thoughts are Plato's scholiasts;

Pater claimed they set the rules of comely form,
And Arnold made their gravity the moral norm.

Now influence, to note, takes two. But ain't it clear
There's less of Greekish fact than English dreaming here?

For influential Greece has no real claim on us.
Influence what way — cure wounds by making pus?

Faint before a fraction? Still, they had, and left,
One really sound idea that still has sap and heft:

Art is imitation. Now the modern mocks,
Parades a thousand wretched canvasses and rocks,

And holds the imitation theory soundly trounced.
But why, of all ideas, is this idea denounced

By charging it with failures it would likewise hoot?
Now Margie is a modern, and is absolute

That imitation's patriarchal and passé.
Expression's her idea; she likes direct display,

And, in older language, favors dash to gust.
Too bad her job's to catalogue, and daily dust,

A thousand little imitative *objets d'art,*
As, a cordial cupboard shaped like Neptune's car,

A lampstand with a palfrey and bashibazouk,
Paperweights of figures from the Pentateuch,

Buxom soft-paste milkmaids, heads of George the Third
In meerschaum and in marble, one-by-one transferred

By Margie to her little bench with breathless care,
Measured, weighed, described, degunked with jets of air,

Swabs and biting solvents, then restored their niche;
A fortune in her fingers, in her judgement — kitsch.

Vexing work, but steady; nay, with speed unslowed
A lifetime's chore at least; some take a day to load,

Some a week to enter and a month to busk.
No wonder Margie's fretted half to death by dusk

And flees to food and musings to disperse her glooms,
Reclining in a spacious set of basement rooms

Provided free of charge, along with board and pay,
By the very dashing owner of those dull *objets.*

With whom she's half in love. That's no surprise, I own;
A lovely girl, a handsome man; a house; alone;

Her hands at servant tasks, romantic mind at play;
He usually, and lately always, home all day;

She hearing him in bed below, at bench above;
Half in love of course. But only half in love!

For Clavering is courteous, and Marge, alas,
Believing this refers to her, and not her class,

Is mystified that warmth unfeigned remains so chill,
And flips between romantic sighs and thwarted will.

Now hearts are like computer chips: they flip and flop
Faster as the temperatures around them drop,

And Margie's jumped as fast, in that near polar cold,
As junctions Japanese that Josephson foretold,

That switch when all resistances have disappeared,
And willingness and willfulness at last cohered.

Perhaps you think this figure slanders human pride?
Myself, I think the chips unfairly villified.

For human beings often stay, and always start,
By nature simply stupid, and progress by art;

So why deny that artifacts begin ahead?
And why not grant the heart to what you grant the head?

Now Margie, compound suffragette and slave, ransacks
Her master's moods and actions, finding much to tax.

Especially she reprehends — if not enjoys —
The way his women callers, with their blatant ploys

And self-revealed venality, are curtly barred.
How dare he treat her sisters with such disregard!

Of course these very ladies had bestowed, before,
Upon the needy Claves as much contempt, or more;

As would have Margie done, had they encountered first
In, say, some social setting, with the roles reversed.

But there's a doubt that even envy can't allay:
What happened to that girl he kept outside all day?

She'd watched her wait, submissive yet withal composed,
Then saw her carried in and heard the suite door closed;

But had she ever left? Or was she still confined?
A mistress? Or was something worse at work behind?

Remember, in New York a courtly carriage shrieks
Of psychopathic, or at least sadistic, streaks;

And Margie, though suburban Boston was her start,
Had quickly learned the local diagnostic art,

And if she sometimes saw the kink before the curl,
Alone — a house — a handsome man — a silly girl

Are circumstances much conducent to such doubt.
And after all, what about that box left out

In front of her apartment, near the service doors?
Did Clavers really think she'd go about her chores

In vinyl miniskirts and scanty cowgirl chaps?
Or were the costumes hers? Or were they his, perhaps?

Of course the clothes in question were the doll's discards,
Which Marge at first repudiates, but soon regards

As one entranced hypnotically, and then submits
To try a vinyl skirt, and finds it almost fits;

And might have started wearing it, had Clavers not
Been summoned for September to his mother's yacht.

So now is Marge alone; and for an afternoon
Works as if her master were nearby. But soon

She haunts the second floor, for those locked doors exert
As much hypnotic power as that vinyl skirt.

Antique bolts are trifles to a jeweller's skill.
She's in, sees nothing, breathes again at ease, until

Around the alcove corner she espies a bed
With one white slender ankle fettered to its stead.

Very white indeed, she notes; in lank repose;
A perfect curve of shin from bated knees to toes;

More perfect still the muscles that enridge the thigh,
The subtle skeins of blue that ward each folded eye,

And open lips fatigued — at once her fears are fled;
She knows it neither drugged, asleep, alive nor dead,

ARNOLD KLEIN

And half-compelled begins to live the moment through:
Undoes each fetter, rubs each limb — a complex cue

Whereby begin abysmal sequences and shunts
Which Burke had not designed but Margie knew at once,

And languidly the widespread leather bracelets grasps,
Enclosing with her skillful hands the silver clasps,

Until submission is the image of release
And somehow very rightly brings us back to Greece:

For clearly Margie called mimesis wholly spent
In ignorance of what it really was, or meant;

Its wretched specimens evoke a like response;
But masterpieces of consummate vraisemblance

Gratify with delectations all their own,
Which Marge had never, till she touched those shackles, known,

And which only grew, by iteration, keen,
And weren't patriarchal in the least, I ween.

At first her calls gave pleasure; then her absence, pang;
Soon she moved upstairs and let her work go hang,

Exploring first the handbook, then each laden shelf,
For though she kept the doll undressed, she dressed herself,

In costumes that demean, reveal, arouse, seduce;
And if they were too tight, too long, too low, too loose,

MONICA

Well, that's between Ms. Leighton and her — love; for whom,
On those brief occasions when she leaves the room,

Margie makes a darling, even dowdy, set
Of wrist and ankle bracelets, with, more precious yet,

Little golden charms in shapes of household things,
And circlets for her ears, and silver pinky rings,

And not a bone or feather in the lot — a choice
Which would have made her old professors' hearts rejoice.

September passes; soon she feels October's breath;
What will happen to her *Bethany*, or Beth,

When Clavering comes back? Will he as well turn Greek,
And, like lame Hephaestus, woven vengeance seek,

Or worse, like insane Ajax, kill, and die of shame?
Or may a man be something more than mad, or lame?

SIX

The frog will fail to snatch the fly that's still or dead;
The tsetse shuns the man and bites the box instead;

For insects and amphibians guide tongue-assaults,
And judge of real and phony, by innate gestalts.

"Lower creatures," yes. But note the step-wise chain:
Frogs spurn flies, and flies scorn men, and men disdain

The real in favor of the fancied; for which lapse
Phrenologists of old invented mental maps

That localized delusions in divided wits.
"Exploded superstition," true; but one that fits

Our 'fatuated friends, whose home's a phrenal chart
In which the upstairs plays the fixed delusion part,

And holds two lower creatures, who, as unawares,
Miss the likely mate who passes up the stairs.

And yet their patterns differ in what each admits.
Clavers doesn't for an instant dream he splits

His lover with his hireling — that pudgy waif;
From whose perspicacity, he's sure, he's safe,

And on whose docile pudginess he soon depends;
For, as fascination bates its tug, he spends

Ever longer hours haunting strange boutiques,
While Margie answers phones, keeps house, and thanks the Greeks.

Perhaps you call it destiny his ardor bates,
But that's as much to do with Burke's design, as Fate's;

It shows how really lifelike his invention was,
To fade a little later than a real girl does,

But mostly that, when passion withers, taste endures;
And here the doll recovers unforeseen allures,

For it doesn't — cannot — baffle Clavers' quirks,
And that has more to do with Fate's design than Burke's,

Who may have made what Clavers wanted, but whose keys
Fashioned not a lover but a wife — love flees,

But marriage lasts, and what can better furnish wives
Than unfagged nonresistance to their partners' drives?

Now Margie, who also has a secret, must defer
To every rare demand the ninny makes on her.

His hours out involve her in such minute cares
That sometimes days are gone before she calls upstairs,

At which poor Margie weeps, and dreams of later trysts;
And which, perhaps, accounts for why her zeal persists,

For such liaisons, snatched and scarce, but slowly pall.
But there's a stronger stale-retardant here withal,

For unlike faded Claves, whose fancies rest on him,
Passive Marge submits her will to someone's whim,

MONICA

Whose variation, with a trillion codes to prime,
Boggles human wits and beggars cosmic time,

For nebulae will flag before repeats appear.
No wonder Margie's sick to see the dawdler clear!

Indeed, she's almost gladder when the ninny's gone
To buy the doll new clothes, than put the old ones on;

For even when she makes it, worlds of worry wait,
For Clavers has a freak, which is, to leave his mate

In close-confining garb and most abjectly trussed,
The better, while he's out, to pique projective lust,

And thus poor Margie never knows, until it haps,
How many hours she will need to clear the straps.

Nor — that done, jewels on, herself abjectly dressed —
How long the doll allows before her pleasures crest;

Its vastitude includes no codes to rush its pace,
As if the cruel-fair doll enjoyed its lover's case,

Which savagery, if real, springs less from programmed rules,
I think, than from the glamour of those household jewels,

For once they're off the domineering cues collapse,
Allowing Marge to rearrange the clothes, and straps.

But that she must do perfectly, lest Clavers guess;
So here's a second world of worry, wide no less,

ARNOLD KLEIN

For Margie must precisely match each arc of pose,
The angle of the ankles where the shackles close,

The taper of the torso from the buttocks' height,
The tension of the pterygoid when bridles bite,

And all this in the aftermath of speedless sex,
With quick surprise impending, not to salt, but vex.

So whether Marge would rather Clavers stays or stirs
Is hard enough to answer, bating jealous spurs;

And these, without believing all the poets' rhymes,
Can goad a Sapphic passion into horrid crimes,

And Margie often contemplates her rival's death;
And might have compassed it, had not one day, from Beth,

I mean from Angie's pointed ear, which he 'gins lick,
Clavers felt an unaccustomed metal tick,

And finds, on close inspection, a forgotten stud,
Which saves his life but rather froze, than spilt, his blood;

And standing back to scan the doll's demeanor marks
A thousand wee divergences in folds and arcs;

And putting it in operation, sees it move
In ways a little languider than he'd approve;

Which makes him, when astonishment wears off, allow
The doll had found a paramour. But who? And how?

That it had free locomotion he flat denied.
And even if it had, he'd kept it bound and tied;

And though as apt as Abelard had been to cede
To *perfectio,* as by inductive need,

Motus, actio and *ens,* he still insists
That even so endowed it can't retie its wrists;

No, that is something someone else would have to do;
And so he turns from asking how to asking who.

The concrete question stumps him. Few suspicions flock;
And then he spies, like husk in hue and hand, a lock,

And recollects the pudge has hair like that in spools;
Has access to the suite; had some dim link with jewels;

Is flesh and blood, an *ens naturae,* in whose brain
Lust and cunning may be safely said to reign;

Is female and *defectus* — here his rants renew,
In which he pounds the girl in every way but two;

And though I don't applaud the theme, and must condemn
His plan to enter Margie's room to match the gem,

I marvel at his breeding, which, in wrath's despite,
Never blames her taste and never vaunts his right;

That is, lets pass unmentioned matters most would hold
As vital to harangue as breathing — lust, and gold.

Now I know illegal search offends the proper creeds.
I'm sure offence attended all of Clavers' deeds;

In fact I wouldn't doubt my own detached reports
Have indifferently disgusted all right-thinking sorts.

But how long could such point-devise precisians preach
Before the themes of lust and gold engulfed their speech?

The unsuspecting Margie proves no cinch to coax.
She stubbornly submits to Clavers' former yokes,

And Clavers too, lest Margie doubt, observes routines,
And docilely departs and conjures dreadful scenes.

Yet Margie's care no further proof of guilt affords,
Though Clavers labors longer with the clothes, and cords;

Indeed her efforts make him doubt, and nigh forbear.
But then her cast-down eyes present her guilty hair,

Her folded hands expose the bracelets of her arms,
Where spatulas and spoons and whisks depend as charms;

And once her hemline chaste above her ankle rode,
Disclosing yet another string of Sapphic code,

Which Clavers, since she never leaves, cannot decrypt;
Till finally, with Marge decoyed abroad, equipt

With owner's key and flashlight, to her rooms he steals,
Unlocks, leans in, turns on, beholds, reflects and — squeals,

For what he sees appals his pride. But more than that,
For next day in the closet of the upstairs flat,

While waiting to surprise the blithe and guilty pudge,
His heart begins to pulse in glee as well as grudge.

For after all those vinyl gleams from Margie's chests
Recalled departed friends and not unwelcome guests;

He couldn't blame the girl for tastes she shared with him;
He couldn't wait to see the doll in vinyl trim;

So lust and curiosity his wrath appease.
But when the waif arrives in vinyl, waist to knees,

Undoes the doll, adorns its ears, and to begin
Assumes the very pose he'd left her lover in,

Lust and curiosity reverse their poles:
He sees he's mastered Margie by remote controls,

A power which, in prospect, almost makes him swoon;
Which was why he fell against the door too soon,

And thus destroyed the prospect and the present views,
For startled Marge by chance reversed the puppet's cues,

Which now begins a deafening, convulsive screech,
Which joined with Margie's shrieks and Clavers' shouts to reach

Even to my garret window 'cross the green;
And so I ended up an actor in their scene.

SEVEN

In Cornwall they describe a man who turned to air.
Tregeagle, whose crimes were such great saints at prayer

Could only win his spirit a respite from Hell
Till he should empty with a leaky limpet shell

Bottomless Dozmare Pool, while demons hoot,
For should he stop his spirit falls to them as loot.

Their vexings leave the ghost aghast; he flees, they chase;
He sees a hermit's hut and through the windowcase

Thrusts his head, and that's asylum of a sort;
His lower half's outside, still prey to demon-sport;

The hermit's prayers are torments too, and he'd pull back,
Except one careless cringe gives Hell the whole to wrack.

Nor anchorite nor imp dislodge the cloven ghost,
Whose interesting screams lay waste the Cornish coast;

The saints convene again, and gain another stay,
While he should plait them ropes of sand to bind the spray

On pounded Padstowe shingle, where the tides unmake
Whatever he can manage for salvation's sake. —

So tedious a chore bored Hell forsook him there,
He wailed alone; wails still: a wind — a man, now air.

Now some say when the Cornish pools are parched, old slimes
Abound in broken shells and hint at secret crimes.

ARNOLD KLEIN

Some, that every noted aspect of the place
Is made a mobile bogey by the Cornish race.

To me, what's represented's neither fact nor lore;
I rather call the tale a Cornish figure for

Poetry —Dozmare lake the Muses' pool,
The leaky limpet language, and the ridicule

Of demons the conditions to a crown of muck,
And call myself Tregeagle for his Cornish luck.

Now my Tregeagle window looked on Clavers' spread;
Indeed, by thrusting out my great Tregeagle head

I could bring each blushless angle of the manse
Within my ungrudged ambit and Tregeagle-glance.

I'd watched while Margie Leighton threaded Clavers' courts,
With folio and case and rolled-up cut-off shorts;

I watched her fingers fidget with an errant twine,
I watched her knot her hair against her little spine,

I saw the sunlight quiver where her feathers shook,
I saw her ring the bell, I saw her leave her nook,

I watched her reappear in vinyl with her love,
Whose advent I had likewise witnessed from above;

For though the errant Burke believed himself unseen,
I watched him lug the doll and then depart serene;

MONICA

I watched the sunbeams profit from its posture still,
I felt the April freeze descend its thighs sans chill;

I saw it brought inside, I watched as passions grew,
I heard their fight begin, and might have watched that too,

Expecting something loving supervene apace
And each exploit the other in the puppet's place,

Or both exploit the doll by turns, or in ménage.
Humane expectation! — And as such, mirage,

For what supervenes is fury, till I asked
Whether there was something big I'd missed, or masked.

Had Claves turned so romantic he shunned womankind?
Had Marge turned gender-keen, who had been object-blind?

He held her straps; she wore his skirt — what kept them chaste?
Or had the loathing more to do with dolls, than taste?

After plastic real discharge might well undo
Not only squeamish Claves but hearty Margie. True,

The doll was wet, but its hydraulic reservoirs
Were easily topped-up from common household jars;

And as for oral ejects, its pneumatic feeds
Were built to answer vocal, and not verbal needs.

Pure airs and waters, then, not salt, and calcite slush,
Which science says compose nine-tenths of human gush,

ARNOLD KLEIN

And make for loathing even 'mongst the doll-less stews.
So why would Marge and Clavers leave the doll, and choose

Partners like themselves, however fit in form?
They oozed and spoke; and worse, as their dispute grew warm,

Screamed and spat; and the thought of shriek and bleed
Made me do the strangest thing of all, a deed.

"Hold!" I shouted, and they did, through mere amaze;
For months they'd thought their dealings hid from human gaze,

And hearing, from above, that sharp, pedantic cry
Made Margie think that God, and Clavers Burke, were by.

Not much as deeds are counted, maybe — just a word,
But the first I'd ever spoken, that the world had heard;

What Oxford dubs a speech-act, rare outside the quads,
But which, by vesting me with Burke's èclat, or God's,

Entered me among them, for our hero, keen
To welcome in the Master to assist his spleen,

Opens without looking first, and in I wend,
A tenant to his eyes, but to his spleen, a friend,

For Claves, supposing males to side against the pudge,
Made sure of my allegiance, and haled me up to judge.

Now it's with men and women as with cats, say I;
Criteria exist until the breedlings vie;

MONICA

With cats, convention posits an idealer plane
From which to judge each breed-specific ideal strain.

The sexes, though, have no such realm to reckon with.
The primal androgyne is merely gnostic myth;

And hypostatic Adam, who contained his wife,
Is a little incommensurate with daily life.

How judge the parties, then, if they possess no par?
I caught close up the common gauge the theorists bar.

Not looks — though only Claves would style Marge a chunk,
Who'd fixed on first appearance, and was puppet-drunk;

For from the way her vinyl droops and spittle hangs
It's as clear she's lost her fat as kept her fangs.

Not rights — for it would be too vulgar to intrude
A standard gentle Claves, with all his wealth, eschewed;

Besides, the issue's *in personam,* not *in rem;*
It isn't ownership, but love, dividing them.

No, *I mean the doll,* for its ideal design
Revealed up close a concrete counter-androgyne,

A sexless thing, remotely girl, but really none,
Through which the genders could, by taking turns, turn one.

The doll was meant to share — and so I might have said
Had Solomon, and not Tregeagle, ruled my head;

ARNOLD KLEIN

For I was like that imp, divided, part and whole,
Between the reason and the corps (and he a soul!),

For I was just as much in love with it as they
And had been since I'd seen it on that April day;

And since their envy put the thought of shares past doubt,
And since, if shares there were, I wanted Clavers out,

I announced, if standing followed gems and clothes,
I came to make a third among them, not compose;

I'd written it a poem, I'd given it a name;
If Clavers had a right, and Margie had a claim,

Why then so did I, which I proposed to press;
True, I'd never touched it, or to deck or dress,

But watching was the nature of the art of verse,
And, among the tastes evinced, the least perverse.

What eloquence began I now let looks conclude.
But, instead of consternation, calm ensued,

For both despised my speech, but saw a way to twine,
And thus triumph, their rival's stronger claims to mine.

But since this role recurred me, as I had myself,
We need some deep decider to dispense the pelf;

So Margie puts on blue jeans and a denim shirt,
And Clavers puts the puppet in a miniskirt,

Replete with pin, in plaid, a sort of kilt-like belt,
White shirt and skinny tie and boots; and he, the svelte

Marge, the punky doll and I by cab depart
To see if Burke possessed, among the rest, this art.

EIGHT

Clavers knew Burke's lair of old; its dusky calms
Give him neither pause nor pleasure, creeps not qualms.

To Margie of the art schools, though, the workshop reeks
Of tiresome ambitions, homework, class critiques.

She's unimpressed by Coptic scrolls and Phillips curves;
The files purse her lips, the femurs try her nerves;

A latent censure wells, for Margie must evade
The thought that Burke and Beth relate as man and made.

She tells herself her pleasure was the puppet's aim,
Without which work was futile, and intention, blame;

And so the luxor yields the prude — the pleasure's prized,
The pains ignored, and he who took the pains, despised,

And by the time the loft's traversed, and Burke appears,
Rising from behind a table, Margie sneers,

For all the many knowledges on which he drew
She deems irrelevant to hers, or means thereto.

The Polyarch's unhabited to scornful use;
Beauty is a thing he makes when moods conduce;

Girls he makes by hand, and youth he blasts at will;
His pride is deep, but Margie's is an oil spill

That spreads itself by thinning — that's what makes pride base;
It barely shares the third of three-dimensioned space,

ARNOLD KLEIN

Yet mere tenuity makes membranes many-hued
That lie an atom thick and are as bad as crude.

But pride, no less than oil, has abyssal dumps
That sometimes reach the surface world in seeps and sumps,

And from Burke's civil nodding even Marge construes
Profundities proportional to surface ooze.

Me, my pearl is modesty, and pearl it is;
I wear it on the inside, like a clam wears his,

In secret self-admiring 'mid the oozy falls;
A little thing, about the size of cannon balls;

Which found itself, however, trumped by Claves' address,
Who limned the situation with such limp finesse

That envy looked in vain for a tendentious word.
So blood will out; for Claves proposed that each be heard

Equally, with Burke to hold the casting straw.
Noblesse indeed! — But not exactly common law,

Especially as Claves considered Burke his man;
But, with all agreeing, the ordeal began.

"A mere lawyer," Claves commenced, "might here contract his brief
To title claims and torts, and gain the law's relief.

But Marshall ruled deep questions on far deeper grounds:
'It is a Constitution that this court expounds!'

He thundered, not a puny writ or contract clause,
But something that itself supplies the ground for laws.

Our dispute's as deep as any Marshall faced.
On what essential ground are all our actions based?

I say it is the heart. This stands for all we prize,
Compassion, intuition, kindness, enterprise,

For virtues are the deeds distilled from vital force,
And naturally derive their symbol from their source.

Thus, as legal rights from legal charters flow,
Lovers' rights from lovers' hearts proceed, and grow,

And judgements arc to hearts that do most deeply pledge.
But how, save from a sign, may we such depths allege?

And which, of lovers' signals, signify the best
But those wherein the animating heart's expressed

In attributes as universal in their kind?
And when we look for these I say its clothes we find.

We need not stay in temperate towns, where all are dressed,
Except to note that culture is thus manifest.

For don't uncitied folk, in deserts and on floes,
Make themselves, from reindeer and from roebuck, clothes?

And even savage clans at ease in jocund zone
Dress themselves in grasses that the winds have sown.

ARNOLD KLEIN

And Neolithic tombs, and barrows of the prime,
Where human nature hovers at the rim of time,

Like shadows in whose errant shape the shape's concealed,
Garments made of leaves, and vines, and treebarks, yield.

And thus we see, in climes extreme, in time and space,
That clothing coincides with, and defines, our race;

And how, when hearts bestow the life they only give,
They clothe the objects of their love, and make them live;

And he who clothes possesses; and the right's to me;
For I have dressed my Angela, as all can see."

"If only," Margie snorted, "we could trace the course
That links these loving threads to their supposed source!

If only love were gravity, whose laws could track
The faintest perturbations of a starbeam back

To some kindly giant sun, known only thus;
If only love, not self-love, were the heart of us!

Astronomers assure us that as black holes spin
They send out pulsing signals, and the heart's akin.

For hearts are self-circumferenced, which wise nature feigns
By tangling them in arteries and venal skeins,

And their throbs are like the noxious rays that surge
From a black hole's rim and catastrophic verge.

What grounds are these for lovers' claims — a static pump
That alternates the thwarting motion with the trump?

A thing, the vertebrate and naked creatures share?
Whose mental correlates are passion and despair?

Since love's defined by reference to another, none;
The words of passive suffering relate to one,

But loving is an action, and as action spurns
Mediating signs and labyrinthine turns,

So love abhors whatever hinders its demands
And habits not the heart but the effecting hands.

For tie, and knot, and bind, as words of loving sort,
Are, in essence, manual, and thus comport;

And fingers made the clothes here made the source of right;
But flaccid fabrics hardly challenge finger-might,

Which proves itself where nature is least prone to yield,
In eons-aged stones and metals thrice-annealed.

The eldest middens archeologists have tapped
Abound in pointed flints that other flints have napped;

Such stonework stands between emergent man and ape;
And metals give the epochs of our culture shape,

As metal-innovation, as with tin, or bronze,
Names the culture-age to which it corresponds.

ARNOLD KLEIN

And eras in which cultures reach refinement's peak,
As China of the Sung and Byzantinish Greek,

Express themselves in minerals and ore combined,
For jewelry is highest of the habile kind

As making, overcoming pertinacious fact,
Things directly consubstantial with the act;

And she who jewels possesses; and the right's to me;
For I have ringed my Bethany, as all can see."

"That a jeweller," I retorted, "might bejewel her belle;
That a millionaire might purchase what the world can sell;

The first afflict our sleeping mother earth for ore,
And stoke telluric fire till the metals roar,

And torment stubborn swages by the mulish peen;
The next compel the wishful winds and frank marine

To bring him spindled sendals in exotic dyes,
Is only what we might expect, and no surprise.

But that the two, though calling on the fourfold stem,
And manifesting biles also, blood, and phlegm,

Should leave the lifeless lifeless yet, is worth remark;
Is there some quintessence missing, some fifth spark,

Some animating other matter may not hold,
That neither millionaire nor maker get by gold,

Whose presence or whose absence settles life and death?
Yes; and it is neither heart nor hand, but breath.

For did not Moses, when he taught the Jews to pray,
In words still found inscribed on hands and hearts today,

In hearts the love of God, on hands the leathern square,
Exalt the breath as life, and more than life, as prayer?

And that Hellenic Moses, Pythagore the Sage,
So divided breath from its corporeal cage

That he taught free transpiration life renewed,
And fed his pupils beans, as being airy food.

And Christian Paul, the skeptic Greekish souls to win,
Made the breath the part that saves from death, and sin.

And that such breath its acme gains in lofty speech,
As discourse, prayer, and sermon, God himself can teach,

Who startled chaos with a word, and as a robe
Wore the winds of earth when he admonished Job.

But among those forms of speech the most sublime,
That sanctify and animate, are song, and rhyme:

Song, because in singing voice is more than voice;
Rhyme, because in rhyming sounds themselves rejoice;

And when these two unite in verse, the lines secure
Not only life, but life eternal, changeless, pure;

ARNOLD KLEIN

And he who sings possesses; and the right's to me;
For I have rhymed my —" and there I had to end my plea,

And leave my verse unsung, for as I spoke I saw
My auditors dilate their pupils, drop their jaw,

Responses hardly suited to my discourse close;
And, though truth can sometimes have effects as gross,

And eloquence eventuate conversion-wise,
I thought it best to turn, and my astonished eyes

Beheld, and pointing to what was its mirror twin,
With hair as red, and ears as sharp, as foil-thin,

As pale, and long, and perfect, dressed and ringed the same,
And yet with something novel in its docile frame,

The puppet come to life, as from a chrysalis.
It stared; it moved; and "Burke," it said, "the fuck is this?"

Astonishment! A second model, better still,
With powers of motility, and voice, and will?

Or the protopuppet Clavers' own excelled?
Consummate or inchoate? Hidden, or withheld?

It all depends on what you wanted, I suppose;
Its ears were pierced, its body seemed to welcome clothes,

Its vulgar language might be meat and drink to some,
And no doubt a cue could make it prim, or dumb.

MONICA

The circumstance, at least, had made such inference plain,
And ardor stirred in Claves', and love in Margie's, brain;

And both approach it wooingly, but it withdraws,
And, cornered, raises, what the doll had not, its claws;

And, hissing, did divulge another trait unique,
Very long incisors, stained like Burmese teak;

And now surprise was down, more deviations out,
As mousey colored roots that leave the red in doubt,

Chains around its shoulders, stockings run to plan,
The kilt a little worn, and from a different clan.

How decrypt this puzzle? Burke provides the gloss:
The girl was real; a punk; his model, and his cross.

His secret model, secret even to herself;
His cross because his girlfriend, an inconstant elf,

A lover of loud nights, girl groups, East Village scenes,
Seventeen years old, from Ozone Park in Queens,

And Ozone was her nickname, but her name was Grace,
Hedonistic, nonchalant, and commonplace.

But not averse, when all had been at length made clear,
To flattery — from Burke, her beauty's engineer,

From Marge, who loved her first in plastic, and from Claves.
These two at once became her living beauty's slaves,

ARNOLD KLEIN

Which settled, in an instant, the disputed swirl:
Burke would keep the puppet, they would take the girl,

Who left the gloomy Polyarch without remorse,
But seemed a little loath to leave the doll, of course,

For she was very sensitive to its allure;
And Clavers gave it back not as a bribe impure,

For the girl was never Burke's to trade, he knew,
But rather out of fear, she'd come to love it too.

And there the story ended! Claves and Marge took Grace
Back to Clavers' mansion, and the puppet's place;

They hung the upper suite with curtains dark and rich;
Two of them got married, but I don't know which;

Burke kept the doll and named it for the vexing punk,
Simplified its circuitry and took its spunk;

And everyone was happy — that is, they pleased themselves.
But time's a little hard on lovers as it delves

And here took half a decade to complete its course,
And *recently it ended in a bad divorce.*

There! Was that the motto I was looking for
To fit this stopwatch town in 1984?

Tregeagle kept his window and his limpet shell;
He labors on forever at Dozmare well;

And though there is no hell that's worse than his, or twin,
With instant Hell ahead whenever labor's in,

Nor any limbo longer, than what leaves in doubt
If endless pains persist when endless pains are out,

Pity him who want to! But even imps, possessed
With one half of dead sin and sharing out the rest,

Allow a poet's better so, and better stuck:
For what is man but water, transience, vice and muck?